MODERN
ITALIAN CUISINE

FOR

EVERYDAY
HOME COOKING

First published in the United States of America in 2022 by
Rizzoli International Publications, Inc.
300 Park Avenue South
New York, NY 10010
www.rizzoliusa.com

Copyright © 2020 Vittorio Assaf and Fabio Granato
Text by Lavinia Branca Snyder
Photography by Mark Roskams
Art direction by Cristina Rizzo

Publisher: Charles Miers
Editor: Daniel Melamud
Design: Sharon Wagner
Copyeditor: Natalie Danford
Proofreader: Tricia Levi
Production Manager: Colin Hough Trapp

Printed in Italy

2022 2023 2024 2025 / 10 9 8 7 6 5 4 3 2 1

ISBN: 978-0-8478-6380-8
Library of Congress Control Number: 2020935296

Visit us online:
Facebook.com/RizzoliNewYork
Twitter: @Rizzoli_Books
Instagram.com/RizzoliBooks
Pinterest.com/RizzoliBooks
Youtube.com/user/RizzoliNY
Issuu.com/Rizzoli

MODERN
ITALIAN CUISINE

FOR

EVERYDAY
HOME COOKING

VITTORIO ASSAF & FABIO GRANATO

TEXT BY LAVINIA BRANCA SNYDER

PHOTOGRAPHY BY MARK ROSKAMS

RIZZOLI
NEW YORK

New York · Paris · London · Milan

TABLE OF CONTENTS

PREFACE

VITTORIO ASSAF AND FABIO GRANATO

This beautiful journey started on a magical day in September 1994. It was a crisp but sunny Labor Day. We were out on Long Island with our girlfriends, and we decided to go sailing. Back then, one of us was definitely not a boat guy—indeed, he was rather skeptical of the sea, but he trusted the other's sailing experience. We left our companions on the beach and embarked on what was supposed to be a quick and relaxed outing. However, it turned out to be quite a different journey—one that almost took our lives and changed our destiny forever.

A few minutes out, the wind picked up to forty miles an hour and our Hobie Cat started to fly over the waves. Some time later a forceful gust snapped the cable holding the mast, and our sail spun around 180 degrees, then tipped forward and sank into the water, pinning our small craft in place. We were too far from shore for anyone to see that we were stranded. We were also too far to see what was happening back on the beach—namely that, unbeknownst to us, our girlfriends had decided to go in for a nap; hours would pass before they noticed that we had failed to return.

Soon daylight started to fade, leaving us helpless. Wave after wave passed over our catamaran; we were wet and cold in the dark. This was in the days before cellphones, so our only hope was to be rescued by a passing craft, or by the Coast Guard.

In order to keep from panicking and to keep ourselves busy, and being the good Italians that we are, we started to talk about food. In the dark, far from shore, helpless and haggard, we recalled dishes that our mothers and grandmothers had prepared on Sundays, like pillowy potato gnocchi, savory eggplant parmigiana, spaghetti dotted with salty bursts of caviar, and silky egg noodles robed in Bolognese sauce. We lovingly recited the details of those beloved favorites. Thinking of home, and of the pleasure of those shared family meals, made the darkness recede and soothed us.

The talk then turned to our dismay that our home, New York City, lacked an authentic, fun Italian restaurant that served that kind of food. Soon we started to fantasize about how such a restaurant would look. We debated what would be on the menu. All the most fabulous Italian regional recipes would be included, we agreed. We detailed how we would modernize the dishes to make them fresh, adding the distinctive touches of Northern Italian and especially Milanese cuisine.

The hours passed, and our situation continued to deteriorate. We were thirsty and hungry and so very cold. We began to fear that we might not make it through the night. It was then, in between one wave and the next, that we made a pact that changed our lives: if we were to survive, we would open the restaurant of our dreams. We'd build a new kind of Italian restaurant in New York, one that served only authentic ingredients. Our restaurant would be a home away from home for our guests and ourselves; it would be an extension of our own kitchens, a beautiful place where friends and acquaintances gathered and found common ground. We shook hands to seal the pact.

It's not an exaggeration to say that pact inspired our will to survive. We held fast, bobbing on our tiny boat, and a few hours later, we were rescued. The rest is history.

We opened our first restaurant exactly one year later, on the second floor at 1022 Madison Avenue at Seventy-ninth Street on Manhattan's Upper East Side. The restaurant served great wines and great food prepared in a tiny kitchen—all at reasonable prices. We even built an authentic wood-burning Neapolitan pizza oven. We flew two experts over from Italy to oversee the process. The oven was constructed of lava stone from Vesuvius and special reclaimed bricks. After ten long days of curing the oven, we fired it up and began producing divine pizza that many say is the best in New York.

At first, not many people believed in us. It was 1995 and no one had ever successfully opened a restaurant on the second floor in a residential neighborhood. But we believed. Our fate had been sealed by that handshake out on the water, and nothing could stop us.

A few weeks after the opening, we found ourselves standing across the street from the restaurant, staring in disbelief at what we had accomplished. There was a line of customers stretching from the second floor all the way out the door. Serafina was the hottest ticket in town. Everyone wanted a table.

In the kitchen our staff was hustling to keep up, and the dining room was full. We spotted members of three different royal families sitting alongside guests who were perhaps not as famous, but were equally important to us. There were kids running everywhere with their mothers chasing after them. Friends of ours filled the tables, along with the kind of cool New Yorkers who show up to check out the latest thing. As we circulated through the room, people waved at us and congratulated us on how marvelous our new restaurant was.

We looked at each other and laughed, "It's wonderful to be restaurateurs!"

PAGE 8: A vintage Moto Guzzi bike and an espresso: the perfect pairing for a great day in Puglia!
ABOVE: A fruit pie, melon, and peaches are served on the garden patio.

Fabio and Vittorio with Jane Goldman, Serafina's visionary landlord, celebrating Serafina's twenty-fifth anniversary.

More than twenty-five years later, we hope that in reading this book you will feel the passion that still drives us to search up and down the Italian peninsula, scouting the best products and discovering artisanal ingredients that make a real difference in our dishes and continue to set Serafina apart.

Italy is a beautiful country, unique in many ways; it is home to wonderful people who work to fulfill their passion and honor their family names. As part of that tradition, we obsessively pursue quality. This means we often visit our producers, many of whom we proudly count among our friends. Finding artisans to partner with us is no easy task. First we have to court them and convince them that we are going to represent them properly. Among those who partnered with us back then and have stayed the course for the past twenty-five years are the Galloni, the Gennari, the De Nigris, the Bindi, and the Banelli/De Sabbata families.

In looking back at the last quarter of a century, a time when we not only launched that first restaurant, but opened new locations in the United States and around the world, we know how lucky we are to have our families' undiminished support and love. We appreciate how they understood and shared the challenges.

Running a restaurant is always a team effort. We want to acknowledge and embrace all of our colleagues and friends who are operating Serafina restaurants around the world. We want to thank them for becoming part of our family and for sharing our passion for quality. It has been a beautiful experience to meet these wonderful people, to have encountered new cultures and been enthusiastically embraced by so many who love the Serafina food and concept.

Serafina has also given us the unparalleled privilege to be surrounded by our guests, to listen and interact with them, to meet new friends every day, to share their conversations, their laughter, their hopes, and their victories.

We would like to dedicate this book to our friends, both guests and partners, and to our families. The more than one hundred recipes in these pages were chosen from among the many we've developed in our kitchen. We believe these dishes will bring the essence of Serafina to you, and we hope you will share our excitement and enthusiasm as you read on.

And finally, no matter where the next twenty-five years take us, we hope to be writing our fiftieth anniversary story with you.

THE
BEAUTY
OF
ITALIAN
COOKING

HERITAGE & INNOVATION

Italy's culinary traditions, especially the country's longstanding farm-to-table philosophy, are the foundation of Serafina restaurants. Those traditions and the idea of seeking out the freshest possible ingredients are behind all the recipes in this book.

Italy was a largely agricultural country for centuries, and Italians remain closely attached to the land and the delicious foods it provides. Leafing through this book, you will be reminded that Italian cooking doesn't call for complex techniques. What it does require is top-quality ingredients that are fresh and offer genuine taste and smell. To preserve those natural qualities, production and preparation techniques that date back centuries are used. That's true whether we're talking about wine, flour, olive oil, vegetables, vinegar, cheese, meat, or fish.

Italian food is a rather new descriptive category. Despite two millennia of shared geography, the Italian peninsula only became a unified state in 1861, and so the country's food remains highly regional. Yet during these two thousand years, the peninsula's inhabitants embraced each other's recipes and products, reworked them into a myriad of variations to accommodate locally available items, and shared them over generations with family and friends. Today on Italian dinner tables across the nation we find such dishes as Bologna's famous tagliatelle, the pizza of Naples, Milanese risotto with saffron, and Foggia's beloved orecchiette pasta.

Italy's geography—wildly varied for a country its size—imbues every ingredient and every dish with a specific regional identity. The island of Ischia sits just miles off the coast of Naples. Inhabitants of the two localities have fished the same waters and shared their histories for centuries. Yet, their food is distinctly different.

This respect for process as well as provenance is reflected in Italian recipes. Our cuisine is based on the premise that each ingredient must shine and make its own contribution. Each is present individually and in the aggregate in the final dish.

PREVIOUS PAGE: Elements of a typical Italian table are set next to bottles of Il Palazzo wine and olive oil.
OPPOSITE PAGE: In Fasano, the ancient olive presses of Puglia's Masseria Borgo San Marco.

CHAPTER 1

ANTIPASTI

THE MODERN ITALIAN ANTIPASTO owes a notable debt to a now legendary cookbook: *Il Cuoco piemontese perfezionato a Parigi* [The Piedmont Cook Perfected in Paris]. The tome in question, first published in 1766, was written by an anonymous eighteenth-century chef who trained in Turin, the capital of Piedmont, then spent several years working in Paris. This author was among the first to encourage Italian *alta cucina* to evolve from a focus on rigid and elaborate French-style recipes to include the use of local and seasonal foods.

No part of the meal is better suited to exemplify that shift in attention, as well as Italy's commitment to its age-old culinary heritage, than the antipasto, or appetizer. With techniques centuries in the making, items such as cured olives and marinated anchovies offer strong flavors and open up the stomach, paving the way for a sensational meal. A platter of thinly sliced prosciutto, beef carpaccio, or bresaola does the same. Stick to the season and offer a few excellent ingredients and you will never go wrong with an antipasto.

CARPACCIO MALATESTA

Carpaccio is very thinly sliced raw beef. The most appropriate cuts of meat are those that have little connective tissue, such as rump, top round, fillet, and sirloin. The best way to get the paper-thin slices you want is to cut the meat with a mechanical slicer when it is very cold. The name carpaccio was invented in 1950 by restaurateur Giuseppe Cipriani. Countess Mocenigo was in town to attend an exhibition of work by the painter Vittore Carpaccio, and her physician had forbidden her from eating cooked meat, so Cipriani fed her a beef carpaccio and a trend was born.

SERVES 4

2 pounds top round beef

1 cup mayonnaise

3 tablespoons Dijon mustard

⅓ cup Pinot Grigio or other white wine

4 cups loosely packed arugula leaves

1 medium carrot, cut into julienne

½ cup Parmigiano Reggiano shavings

2 lemons, cut into wedges

Carefully slice the top round beef as thinly as possible.

In a small bowl, whisk the mayonnaise with the mustard and the wine until you obtain a smooth sauce. Place the sliced filet mignon on a platter in a single layer. Drizzle as much sauce as you like on top. [You may not need all of the sauce. It will keep, covered, in the refrigerator for several weeks.] Form the arugula leaves and carrot into a mound in the center of the platter and arrange the shaved Parmigiano Reggiano on top of the salad. Garnish with lemon wedges.

FILET MIGNON CARPACCIO WITH TRUFFLES

Truffles are edible fungi that grow chiefly in leafy woodlands. The black summer truffle (Tuber aestivum) is found across Europe. The Burgundy truffle (designated Tuber uncinatum) is harvested in the autumn. Tuber magnatum is the most highly prized truffle, a white truffle that is found mainly in northern Italy in the countryside around the cities of Alba and Asti, as well as in Molise.

SERVES 4

3 medium potatoes
Salt to taste
1 tablespoon unsalted butter
½ cup whole milk
7 ounces black summer truffle
2 pounds filet mignon, very thinly sliced
Flat-leaf parsley sprigs for garnish
Freshly ground black pepper to taste

Place the potatoes in a pot of cold salted water and bring to a boil. Cook the potatoes until they are tender enough to pierce with a paring knife, then drain, peel, and quarter. Dice one of the potato quarters and set aside. Place the other 11 potato quarters in a large bowl.

Place the butter and milk in a saucepan and place over low heat. Cook, stirring occasionally, until the butter has melted. Gradually and slowly pour the milk and butter into the potatoes in a thin stream while mashing the potatoes. Continue until the potatoes are creamy and pourable. Shave the truffle and stir it into the mashed potatoes. Allow the potatoes to cool to room temperature. Fold in the reserved diced potato.

Arrange the thinly sliced filet mignon on individual plates or a platter. Drizzle the truffle sauce on top and garnish with the parsley. Season to taste with black pepper.

ARTICHOKE CARPACCIO WITH SHRIMP

In this recipe, the soft texture and sweet flavor of the shrimp contrast with the crunch and slightly bitter flavor of the artichokes for ideal balance. The best artichokes grow in early spring.

SERVES 4

1½ cups freshly squeezed lemon juice

6 large artichokes

1 cup orange juice

24 medium shrimp, shelled and deveined

¼ cup plus 1 tablespoon extra-virgin olive oil

Leaves of 1 sprig flat-leaf parsley, minced

5 cloves garlic, minced

⅓ cup Pinot Grigio or other white wine

Chopped tomatoes for garnish

Salt to taste

Freshly ground black pepper to taste

Basil leaves for garnish

Prepare a large bowl of cold water and ½ cup lemon juice. Prepare the artichokes by removing the outer leaves and the chokes so that only the hearts remain. As you clean the artichokes, drop them into the prepared bowl of water to prevent them from browning. When all the artichokes have been prepared, combine the remaining 1 cup lemon juice and the orange juice in another bowl. Thinly slice the artichoke hearts and toss them with the orange juice mixture.

In a frying pan, sauté the shrimp in 1 tablespoon olive oil with the parsley and garlic. Add the white wine and let it evaporate. Plate the artichoke slices and put the shrimp and their sauce on top of the artichokes, then garnish with chopped tomatoes, season with salt and black pepper, garnish with shredded basil leaves, and drizzle on the remaining ¼ cup olive oil.

CARPACCIO OF SMOKED SALMON WITH DILL

Dill pairs well with many types of seafood, but it really shines when paired with salmon. The contrasting textures and flavors really make this dish. The ingredients complement one another while still presenting their own distinct tastes and aromas.

SERVES 4

1 small red onion

16 slices Norwegian smoked salmon

2 teaspoons capers in vinegar, rinsed and drained

2 to 3 drops truffle oil, optional

1 sprig dill

3 lemon slices

Freshly ground black pepper to taste

Thinly slice the onion and place the rings in the middle of a platter. Place the salmon slices in a single layer around the onion and scatter the capers on the salmon. Sprinkle on the truffle oil, if using. Garnish with the dill. Cut each lemon slice from the outer edge to the center, then twist the slices and arrange them on the plate. Season with black pepper and serve.

CARPACCIO OF TUNA WITH GINGER & AVOCADO

Traditionally carpaccio is thinly sliced beef, but we like to make this delicate dish with seafood and even vegetables. This Asian-flavored version is a Serafina favorite. Ginger simmered in grenadine turns bright red and slightly sweet.

SERVES 4

1½ pounds fresh tuna

Freshly ground black pepper to taste

1 tablespoon extra-virgin olive oil

1 2-inch piece of ginger, peeled

About ½ cup grenadine

½ cup plus 2 tablespoons soy sauce

½ cup plus 2 tablespoons toasted
    sesame oil

1 avocado

1 bunch watercress

1 tablespoon plus 1 teaspoon
    sesame seeds

Coat the tuna with a generous amount of black pepper. Place a frying pan over high heat and when it is very hot add the olive oil. Quickly sear the tuna. Remove and allow to cool to room temperature, then freeze until firm.

Meanwhile, cut the ginger into julienne and place it in a saucepan with ½ cup grenadine and ¼ cup water. If the liquid doesn't cover the ginger, add grenadine until it does. Bring to a boil, then simmer until the ginger is soft and bright red, 10 to 15 minutes.

In a small bowl, mix the soy sauce and the sesame oil.

Once the tuna is firm, remove it from the freezer and cut it into thin slices with a sharp knife or a food slicer and plate it. Arrange the ginger on top of the tuna. Pit, peel, and slice the avocado and arrange the avocado slices on top of the ginger. Scatter on sprigs of watercress and the sesame seeds. Serve the prepared soy sauce and sesame oil mixture on the side.

TARTARE DI SOFIA

Crudo, meaning raw, is Italy's answer to sushi and is served up and down the Italian coastline. Tuna tartare was created in 1980 by a Japanese chef based in California. This is our Serafina version, with a nod to old and new.

SERVES 4

⅓ cup extra-virgin olive oil

1 piece ginger, sliced

1 shallot, sliced

1 pound fresh tuna

½ cup mayonnaise

1 tablespoon Dijon mustard

3 tablespoons chopped parsley

1 pound fresh salmon

6 cherry tomatoes, halved

12 croutons

12 thin lemon slices

12 thin cucumber slices

Dill for garnish

Make a flavored oil by combining the olive oil, ginger, and shallot. Puree the mixture in a blender and then refrigerate for 8 hours. Strain the oil through a sieve before using.

Chop the tuna into small dice, mix it with 2 tablespoons of the mayonnaise, the mustard, and half of the parsley. Separately chop the salmon and mix with 2 tablespoons of the mayonnaise and the remaining parsley. Use a ring mold to make a disk of about one quarter of the salmon mixture on an individual plate. With the ring mold still in place, top with about one quarter of the tuna mixture and smooth the top. Carefully remove the ring mold and repeat with the remaining tuna and salmon to make 4 disks of two layers each on 4 individual plates. Garnish the tartare with the tomatoes, croutons, lemon slices, and cucumber slices. Drizzle the remaining mayonnaise onto the plates. Add a drizzle of the oil flavored with ginger and shallot to each serving. Garnish each disk of tuna and salmon with dill.

TUNA BRUSCHETTA

Bruschetta is a rustic dish found throughout the Italian peninsula under a variety of local names.
The foundation is always the same: toasted bread flavored with garlic, olive oil, and salt. Bruschetta
may be topped with tomatoes, cheese, sautéed mushrooms, or—as it is here—fish.

SERVES 4

1 red onion

**10 ounces canned tuna in olive oil,
  drained and flaked**

Salt to taste

Freshly ground black pepper to taste

1 baguette

**Extra-virgin olive oil for brushing and
  drizzling**

1 lemon, cut into wedges

Preheat the oven to 400°F. Finely chop the onion. Mix the tuna with the onion and a pinch of salt and black pepper.

Slice the baguette. Brush the slices on both sides lightly with oil. Spread the bread slices in a single layer on a cookie sheet or jelly-roll pan and toast in the preheated oven until golden, about 10 minutes. Let the bread cool for 5 minutes, then spoon the tuna mixture onto the toasted bread. Drizzle with olive oil and garnish with lemon wedges.

CARCIOFI ALLA ROMANA

Roman cuisine evolved over two thousand years, starting when the city was the capital of a vast empire that stretched from England to the Middle East. This long-lasting empire exposed Roman citizens to foreign culinary habits and new cooking techniques. In the more recent past, some five hundred years ago, when the Vatican was at the peak of its power, Rome became the place where the best chefs of Europe were employed, and people such as Bartolomeo Scappi further elevated Roman cuisine.

SERVES 4

Freshly squeezed juice of 1 lemon

4 large artichokes

2 to 3 garlic cloves

2 to 3 sprigs flat-leaf parsley

7 to 8 black olives

½ cup white wine

2 tablespoons extra-virgin olive oil

Prepare a large bowl of cold water and the lemon juice. Prepare an artichoke by removing the outer leaves but leaving the stem attached. Cut in half lengthwise and remove the exposed choke. Drop the artichoke into the prepared bowl of water to prevent it from browning. Repeat with the remaining artichokes.

Place the artichokes and all the remaining ingredients in a large pot and add water to cover. Bring to a boil and then simmer until the artichokes are tender, about 40 minutes. Drain the artichokes, discarding the other ingredients.

PORCINI TRIFOLATI

Porcini mushrooms have a distinctive nutty flavor. They are relatively rare because they engage in a special symbiotic relationship with the roots of plants that makes them hard to cultivate. The name of this dish means porcini mushrooms thinly sliced and sautéed.

SERVES 4

2 pounds porcini mushrooms

2 to 3 garlic cloves

¼ cup extra-virgin olive oil

1 cup chopped flat-leaf parsley

Crushed red pepper to taste

Thinly slice the mushrooms. Chop the garlic cloves.

In a skillet, heat 3 tablespoons of the olive oil. Sauté the garlic over medium heat until browned, 2 to 3 minutes, then add the mushrooms and turn the heat to high. Add ¾ cup parsley and some crushed red pepper. Cook, stirring, over high heat until the mushrooms have given up their liquid and begin to brown, 4 to 5 minutes. [If you prefer more tender mushrooms, cook them over medium-low heat for 8 to 10 minutes until soft.] Remove from heat and add the remaining ¼ cup parsley and drizzle with the remaining 1 tablespoon olive oil.

ARANCINI WITH MEAT

This signature Sicilian street food dates to the period between the ninth and eleventh centuries when Arabs dominated the island; per the Arab manner, rice and meat were picked up by hand and rolled into a ball for consumption. Even on Sicily there are variations. In and around Palermo, these are round balls, while on the eastern side of Sicily they are more cone-shaped.

MAKES 14 TO 18 ARANCINI

5 pounds beef or chicken bones or a combination of the two

2 carrots

3 small yellow onions

2 ribs celery

1 sprig flat-leaf parsley

¼ cup plus 2 tablespoons extra-virgin olive oil

1 pound (about 2⅓ cups) arborio rice

1 generous pinch saffron

½ cup white wine

1 pound ground beef

Salt to taste

Freshly ground black pepper to taste

5 ounces mozzarella, drained and diced

Olive oil for frying

2 large eggs

2 cups breadcrumbs

Place the bones in a stockpot. Add the carrots, 1 onion, the celery, and parsley. Add water to cover. Bring to a boil, then cover with a tight-fitting lid and reduce the heat to a gentle simmer. Simmer for 3 to 4 hours, occasionally removing foam with a skimmer. Add hot water to keep the ingredients submerged, if needed. When the broth is ready, strain it through a cheesecloth-lined colander or strainer, then return it to the pot. Bring to a simmer over low heat.

Chop 1 onion and heat 3 tablespoons of olive oil in a saucepan. Sauté the chopped onion for 2 minutes, then add the rice. Sauté, stirring constantly, for 2 additional minutes, then add the saffron and the wine. Continue to cook, stirring frequently, and when the wine has been absorbed by the rice, add about ½ cup of the warm stock to the saucepan. Simmer, stirring constantly, until most of the broth has been absorbed, then add another ½ cup of broth. Continue stirring and adding stock when the previous addition has been absorbed, decreasing the amount added slightly each time. Repeat until the rice is cooked al dente, then remove from the heat and set aside to cool.

Chop the remaining onion and heat the remaining 3 tablespoons olive oil in a saucepan. Sauté the chopped onion for 2 minutes, then add the ground beef with a pinch of salt and black pepper. Sauté until browned, stirring frequently and breaking up any large chunks of meat. Once the meat is completely browned, remove from the heat. In a bowl combine the meat and cheese and mix to combine.

In a deep fryer or a pot with high sides, heat the frying oil to 350°F. Line sheet pans with paper towels and set aside.

Pick up some rice and shape it into a ball 1½ inches in diameter. Press your finger into the center, then fill the indent with a little of the meat and cheese mixture. Pinch the rice around the filling to enclose it. Repeat with the remaining rice and filling.

Whisk the eggs in a shallow bowl. Place the breadcrumbs in a separate bowl. Dredge a rice ball first in egg and then in breadcrumbs to coat on all sides. Repeat with the remaining rice balls.

Fry the arancini in batches, turning them often, until golden, 2 to 3 minutes. Remove from the oil with a slotted spoon or skimmer and place on the prepared pans to drain briefly. Season with salt and serve hot.

CHAPTER 2

SALADS

THERE ARE LITERALLY HUNDREDS of salads in the Italian culinary repertoire that are referred to either as *insalatine*, small salads, or *insalate*, salads. *Insalatine* include dishes entirely dedicated to raw vegetables, often leafy lettuces, such as greens in the endive and chicory family and *misticanza*, or mixed mesclun greens. Some examples are *insalata tricolore* in the colors of the Italian flag and *insalata mista*—lettuce with a tuft of grated carrots and some radishes or tomatoes. In Italy most leafy greens are produced in Puglia, Campania, Lazio, Abruzzo, and Sicily. These salads—which you can adapt to your taste—are almost always dressed with a combination of olive oil, salt, and either lemon juice or vinegar. They are typically served as accompaniments.

 Insalate can be composed of only raw vegetables or may be more structured dishes, often with protein or grains incorporated. These salads may stand as one-dish meals or be shared as an antipasto. We especially like a big salad as a main course on a hot summer day. Passing around a platter and letting guests serve themselves highlights the communal feeling behind every Italian meal.

TRICOLORE SALAD

An *insalata tricolore* is a salad in the three colors of the Italian flag: green, white, and red. The green is usually green lettuce, basil, or arugula. The red is radicchio or tomato. Belgian endive, fennel, or mozzarella contributes the white.

SERVES 4

2 heads Romaine lettuce

2 small heads radicchio, preferably the red Verona variety

2 bulbs fennel

Extra-virgin olive oil to taste

Red or white balsamic vinegar to taste

Salt to taste

Freshly ground black pepper to taste

Chop the Romaine lettuce and the radicchio. Cut the fennel into quarters. Toss in a large salad bowl, then dress with olive oil, vinegar, salt, and black pepper to taste and toss to combine.

PORTO CERVO SALAD

Porto Cervo is a gorgeous seaside town on the northern coast of the island of Sardinia. You might be surprised to see corn, which is native to the Americas, in an Italian salad, but it's quite popular in Italy. Spanish settlers and traders brought corn to Europe from their journeys to the New World. Over the next four centuries corn's ability to grow in diverse climates, its resiliency, and the lack of taxation during the Renaissance led to widespread adoption of corn by both Southern and Northern Italian culinary cultures. Of course, corn is also commonly dried and ground into polenta.

SERVES 4

2 heads Romaine lettuce

4 carrots

2 small avocados

1 15-ounce can corn, drained

¼ cup Dijon mustard

Freshly squeezed juice of ½ lemon

¼ cup extra-virgin olive oil

¼ cup white wine

3 tablespoons balsamic vinegar

½ cup heavy cream

Salt to taste

Freshly ground black pepper to taste

Chop the lettuce. Cut the carrots into julienne. Pit and peel the avocados and slice thinly. In a large salad bowl combine the lettuce, carrots, avocado, and corn.

In a small bowl, whisk the mustard, lemon juice, olive oil, wine, vinegar, and cream until smooth. Season to taste with salt and black pepper. Drizzle the dressing over the salad. (You may not need all of it. Any leftover dressing will keep, covered, in the refrigerator for several days. Whisk to combine before using.) Toss the salad with the dressing and serve.

BEET SALAD WITH PISTACHIOS

The beet has been credited with medicinal virtues since the Middle Ages. It was appreciated by no less than Italian Renaissance author and gastronomist Bartolomeo Sacchi (known as Platina), author of the first printed cookbook, *De honesta voluptate et valetudine* [On Honest Pleasure and Good Health]. This forerunner of the lifestyle cookbook combines recipes with philosophical advice. It was published in Rome in 1474.

SERVES 4

3 large beets

2 loosely packed cups arugula

2 heads Belgian endive, chopped

8 ounces goat cheese

¾ cup pistachios

Extra-virgin olive oil for dressing

Salt to taste

Freshly ground black pepper to taste

Bring a large pot of [unsalted] water to a boil and cook the beets until tender, about 30 minutes. Remove from the heat and drain. You may want to wear gloves when working with beets, as they can stain your hands [as well as your cutting board and counter]. When the beets are cool enough to handle, peel them and thinly slice them. Arrange the slices on a platter. Combine the arugula and endive and mound the greens on the platter. Slice the goat cheese into disks and arrange them on top of the greens, then scatter on the pistachios. Dress with olive oil, salt, and black pepper.

AVOCADO & BRUSSELS SPROUT SALAD

The pairing of Brussels sprouts with Parmigiano Reggiano is a classic. The number of variations on this theme is a testament to how well these opposites attract. In this dish, the mild avocado allows their flavors and textures to shine beautifully.

SERVES 4

1 pound Brussels sprouts

1 clove garlic

1 tablespoon plus 1½ teaspoons vegetable oil

1½ teaspoons olive oil

Salt to taste

Freshly ground black pepper to taste

4 avocados

Juice of ½ lemon

1 cup grated Parmigiano Reggiano

¼ cup Parmigiano Reggiano shavings

Leaves of 1 head Belgian endive

1 lemon, thinly sliced

Chop the Brussels sprouts (core them if the cores are large and woody) and steam them for 2 minutes just to soften them slightly—you do not want to cook them. Then sauté the garlic in the two types of oil until browned, remove and discard the garlic, and sauté the steamed Brussels sprouts for 2 minutes. Season with salt and black pepper. Set aside to cool, then chop.

Pit, peel, and dice the avocados and toss with the Brussels sprouts; add lemon juice and grated Parmigiano and toss gently to combine. Use a ring mold to make disks of the Brussels sprout mixture on individual plates. Top each disk with Parmigiano shavings. Garnish with endive leaves and lemon slices.

CAESAR SALAD WITH CHICKEN

Some sources attribute the invention of Caesar salad to an Italian immigrant in Chicago who named the dish after the Roman emperor. Others believe it was an Italian immigrant in Tijuana named Caesar Cardini, who first served the salad in his namesake restaurant in the 1920s to well-to-do Americans who traveled to Mexico to imbibe during Prohibition. Cardini's guests included a young girl by the name of Julia McWilliams—better known by her married name, Julia Child—and Wallis Simpson, the future wife of Prince Edward VIII.

SERVES 4

2 boneless skinless chicken breasts
½ cup plus 2 tablespoons extra-virgin olive oil
Salt to taste
Freshly ground black pepper to taste
10 anchovy fillets, rinsed
About 1 cup white wine vinegar
5 cups loosely packed basil leaves
1⅓ cups pine nuts
1 clove garlic
1⅔ cups grated Parmigiano Reggiano
3 egg yolks
1 head Romaine lettuce
Focaccia for serving

Pound the chicken breasts to an even thickness with a meat mallet. In a shallow dish, combine 3 tablespoons of the olive oil with salt and black pepper. Place the chicken breasts in the dish, turn to coat, cover, and marinate in the refrigerator for 1 hour. While the chicken is marinating, soak the anchovy fillets in vinegar to cover.

In a blender puree the basil, pine nuts, garlic, ¼ cup plus 1 tablespoon olive oil, and a pinch of salt until smooth. Then add ⅔ cup grated Parmigiano and blend until thickened. Set aside.

Drain the anchovies and mince them. In a bowl whisk together the minced anchovies, egg yolks, and remaining 1 cup grated Parmigiano until thick and well-combined.

Heat the remaining 2 tablespoons olive oil in a skillet over medium-high heat, then remove the chicken from the marinade and cook until opaque in the center and lightly browned on the surface, about 5 minutes per side. Let the chicken cool for 5 minutes, then cut into strips.

Shred the Romaine lettuce. In a bowl, toss the shredded lettuce, the anchovy mixture, and the chicken until combined. Arrange the salad on individual plates and include a slice or two of focaccia with each serving. Drizzle the basil sauce around the rim of each plate.

ARUGULA & FILETTO SALAD

This classic dish allows both the tender, sweet beef and the peppery arugula to shine brightly, as their flavors are layered but not comingled.

SERVES 4

2 pounds filet mignon

Extra-virgin olive oil for sautéing and dressing

Salt to taste

Freshly ground black pepper to taste

7 ounces arugula

16 cherry tomatoes

½ cup Parmigiano Reggiano shavings

Leaves of 1 small head Belgian endive

Slice the filet mignon. In a skillet, heat some olive oil and cook the filet to your preferred doneness. Season with salt and black pepper.

In a bowl, toss the arugula with the cherry tomatoes. Dress with a little olive oil, toss to combine, then arrange in the center of a platter. Top the arugula with Parmigiano shavings, then arrange the filet mignon and the endive leaves on the platter.

SPAGHETTI WITH GRATED BOTTARGA

Bottarga is fish roe that is salted and dried. It is sold as whole roe sacs that must then be grated or shaved. It is powerful and pungent, with a strong hit of umami flavor. Mullet bottarga is produced mainly in Sardinia and parts of Tuscany, while tuna bottarga is found in Sicily, Sardinia, and Reggio Calabria. When bottarga is grated over spaghetti (rather than shaved), the savory and briny flecks wrap around the shaft of each piece and the flavor is thus well distributed and delivered evenly in every bite.

SERVES 4

Salt to taste

1 pound thin spaghetti

½ cup extra-virgin olive oil

2 to 3 ounces bottarga

Bring a large pot of salted water to a boil and cook the pasta until al dente. Drain in a colander.

In a skillet, heat the olive oil over medium heat. Toss the spaghetti with the oil for 1 minute.

Divide the pasta among individual serving bowls and finish by grating bottarga on top.

SPAGHETTI WITH CALAMARI, BOTTARGA & MUSSELS

Pasta with seafood is often topped with a scattering of crisp breadcrumbs or a sprinkling of grated bottarga.

SERVES 4

16 green mussels

2 cloves garlic, minced

1 tablespoon extra-virgin olive oil

½ pound squid, chopped

½ cup white wine

16 cherry tomatoes, quartered

Salt to taste

1 pound thin spaghetti

2 ounces bottarga

Freshly ground black pepper to taste

½ cup minced parsley

Wash the mussels in several changes of water, pull off any beards, and scrub the shells. Discard any mussels with broken shells. In a large skillet, sauté the garlic in the olive oil over medium heat. Add the squid, mussels, and wine.

Cover and cook briefly until all the mussels have opened. Remove the meat from the shells and return to the pan. Discard any unopened mussels. Add the tomatoes and cook until they collapse.

Meanwhile, bring a large pot of salted water to a boil and cook the pasta until al dente. Drain and toss in the skillet for 1 minute, then divide the pasta among individual serving bowls. Grate bottarga over the pasta, then season with black pepper and scatter on the parsley.

PENNE ALLA SALVIA

Penne is one of the few pasta shapes whose origins are well documented. In 1865, a pasta producer by the name of Giovanni Battista Capurro patented a new machine. The revolutionary device was able to cut pasta diagonally without squashing it, and it could be set to cut the tubes in varying lengths. Penne rigate are lined with ridges that trap this luscious butter sauce.

SERVES 4

Salt to taste

1 pound penne rigate

2 sticks plus 4 tablespoons unsalted butter

Leaves of 1 sprig sage

1 cup grated Parmigiano Reggiano

Bring a large pot of salted water to a boil and cook the pasta until al dente.

Meanwhile, melt the butter over medium heat in a large skillet. Reserve a few of the prettier sage leaves for garnish, then add the remaining leaves to the skillet with the melted butter and sauté until the butter turns golden and sage is fragrant.

When the pasta is done, drain in a colander, then add to the skillet and toss over medium heat until combined, about 2 minutes. Divide the pasta among individual serving bowls. Garnish with the reserved sage and sprinkle on the Parmigiano.

PASTA E FAGIOLI

There are few dishes more satisfying than a hearty bowl of pasta with beans, yet another dish present in different regions of Italy in different forms. You can play with this recipe any way you like by using different types of beans, seasonal vegetables, and a variety of pasta shapes—just be sure to use short pasta. If all you have is long pasta such as spaghetti, break it into short lengths. This can be a very brothy soup or a more dense dish, depending on how much water you add.

SERVES 4

2 tablespoons extra-virgin olive oil, plus more for drizzling

1 yellow onion, diced

1 carrot, diced

1 plum tomato, diced

2 15-ounce cans pinto beans, drained and rinsed

Salt to taste

10 ounces ditali or other short pasta

½ cup grated Parmigiano Reggiano

Freshly ground black pepper to taste

Heat 2 tablespoons olive oil in a large saucepan over medium-high heat. Add the onion, carrot, and tomato and sauté until softened, 2 to 3 minutes. Add the beans and 2 to 6 cups water, depending on how brothy you would like the finished dish to be. Reduce the heat to low and let the beans simmer.

Meanwhile, bring a large pot of salted water to a boil and cook the pasta until not quite al dente. Drain and add to the simmering beans and continue cooking until the pasta is done.

Divide the pasta among individual soup bowls and top with grated Parmigiano. Season with salt and black pepper and add an additional drizzle of extra-virgin olive oil atop each portion.

TAGLIATELLE WITH PEAS, POTATOES & PESTO

Tagliatelle are egg noodles that are wider than fettuccine but more narrow than pappardelle. It is a versatile pasta that marries well with vegetables, meat sauces, and even seafood options. This recipe is a classic piatto povero, a category of dishes based on inexpensive everyday seasonal produce available in neighborhood markets and home gardens.

SERVES 4

1 medium potato

¼ cup plus 2 tablespoons extra-virgin
   olive oil

1¾ cups frozen peas, thawed

5 cups basil leaves

1¾ cups pine nuts

1 clove garlic

Salt to taste

3 ounces Parmigiano Reggiano

1 pound tagliatelle

Bring a small pot of water to a boil and boil the potato until it is easily pierced with a paring knife, about 15 minutes. Drain, and when it is cool enough to handle, peel and dice it. Heat 1 tablespoon of the olive oil in a small skillet and warm the peas.

In a blender combine the basil, 1½ cups pine nuts, garlic, the remaining ¼ cup plus 1 tablespoon olive oil, and a pinch of salt. Blend until smooth, with only a few green flecks left. Then add 2 ounces of the Parmigiano Reggiano and blend until thick.

Bring a large pot of salted water to a boil and cook the pasta until al dente. Drain the pasta and in a large serving bowl toss with the pesto, diced potato, and peas. Scatter on the remaining ¼ cup pine nuts and grate the remaining 1 ounce Parmigiano over the pasta.

TAGLIOLONI CORTINA

Cortina d'Ampezzo is a fashionable ski resort in the Dolomites. This dish of egg noodles, pasta, and prosciutto is just the type of hearty fare you want after a day on the slopes.

SERVES 4

Salt to taste

1 pound tagliolini

¼ cup extra-virgin olive oil

1 7-ounce slab prosciutto, cut into strips

2 portobello mushrooms, chopped

1½ cups frozen peas

2 tablespoons heavy cream (optional)

Freshly ground black pepper to taste

1 cup grated Parmigiano Reggiano

Bring a large pot of salted water to a boil and cook the pasta until al dente.

Place the olive oil in a large skillet over medium heat. When the oil is hot add the prosciutto, mushrooms, and peas. If using, add the cream to the skillet as well.

Sauté until the mushrooms and peas are soft, about 5 minutes.

When the pasta is al dente, drain and add to the skillet. Toss over medium heat to combine, about 1 minute. Divide the pasta among individual serving bowls. Season with black pepper and pass grated Parmigiano on the side.

PASTA ALLA MARTINO

Unlike bacon, pork belly that is cold-smoked after being cured, Italian pancetta is simply cured with salt and spices. Pancetta adds subtle richness to this perfect fall dish. The name is a reference to the summer of San Martino—the days in November when the weather turns unusually balmy.

SERVES 4

Salt to taste

1 pound tagliolini

2 tablespoons unsalted butter

½ red onion, sliced

1 tablespoon green peppercorns

3½ ounces pancetta, cut into strips

½ cup minced chives

Bring a large pot of salted water to a boil and cook the pasta until al dente.

Melt the butter in a large skillet over high heat. Add the onion and green peppercorns and sauté until the onion is soft. Add the pancetta strips and cook until the pancetta is translucent but not crispy, 3 to 4 minutes.

When the pasta is al dente, drain and add it to the skillet. Toss over medium heat to combine, about 1 minute. Divide the pasta among individual serving bowls and sprinkle on the minced chives.

PAPPARDELLE ALLA BOLOGNESE

Pappardelle are wide egg noodles, typically about 1 inch across. They work well with thicker sauces, such as this Bolognese. They are also frequently paired with game, such as wild boar or venison.

SERVES 4

1 tablespoon extra-virgin olive oil

2 medium yellow onions, minced

10 ounces ground beef

10 ounces ground veal

4 dried bay leaves

2 tablespoons dried oregano

1 cup red wine

Salt to taste

Freshly ground black pepper to taste

1 15-ounce can diced tomatoes

1 pound pappardelle

1 cup grated Parmigiano Reggiano

1 fresh bay leaf for garnish

Heat the olive oil in a large saucepan over medium-high heat. Add the onions and sauté until golden and soft. Add the ground beef and veal. Sauté until browned, stirring often and breaking up any large chunks with a fork. Once the meat is completely browned, add the 4 bay leaves, oregano, and wine. Season with salt and black pepper, then increase the heat to a brisk simmer and cook until the wine has evaporated. Add the tomatoes. Reduce the heat as low as possible, so that it is barely simmering, cover, and simmer gently for 2 hours. Occasionally stir and check that the sauce is not drying out. If it begins to look dry, add water in small amounts, but it should be dense.

Bring a large pot of salted water to a boil and cook the pasta until al dente. Drain and transfer to a large serving bowl. Top the pasta with the Bolognese sauce and toss to combine. Divide the pasta among individual serving bowls and garnish with bay leaves. Serve the grated Parmigiano on the side.

9 Cut the dough into noodles: pappardelle are ¾ to 1 inch wide; tagliatelle are about ⅓ inch wide; fettuccine are about ¼ inch wide. For ravioli, you will want strips about 1½ inches wide.

10 Unfurl the noodles and separate them.

11 Tousle the noodles with a little flour and let them dry at room temperature briefly.

RAVIOLI ALLA SALVIA

The ancient stuffed *raviolus* reached Parma from Genoa before the end of the thirteenth century. A century later poet Giovanni Boccaccio elevated the status of ravioli by name-checking them in *The Decameron*. Stuffed pillows of pasta have been beloved ever since. Don't be nervous about making your own egg pasta—it's not difficult. But do be sure to let the dough rest for thirty minutes so it relaxes. If you try to skimp on the resting time, you won't be able to roll out the dough thin enough no matter how hard you try, and the resulting ravioli will be gummy. The melted butter and sage topping is a classic one for ravioli.

SERVES 4

3¾ cups unbleached all-purpose flour

1½ teaspoons grated nutmeg

3 egg yolks

1 pound baby spinach

10 ounces ricotta

1½ cups grated Parmigiano Reggiano

Salt to taste

Freshly ground black pepper to taste

1 large egg, well beaten

3 tablespoons unsalted butter

Leaves of ½ bunch sage, chopped
   if very large

Shape the flour and ½ teaspoon of the grated nutmeg into a well on the work surface. Place the egg yolks in the center and beat them with a fork. Begin pulling flour in from the sides of the well with the fork until you have a crumbly dough. Using your hands and a bench scraper, if necessary, continue kneading until you have a smooth, soft, compact dough. Adjust dryness with small amounts of flour or water if necessary. Shape the dough into a ball, wrap it or cover it, and set aside to rest for 30 minutes.

Meanwhile, prepare the filling. In a pot, cook the baby spinach in a small amount of water until wilted. Drain well, pressing the spinach against the sides of a colander or sieve, then purée with a food mill, letting it drop into a bowl. Add the ricotta, the remaining 1 teaspoon of nutmeg, and ½ cup of the grated Parmigiano. Season with salt and black pepper and stir to combine.

Using a rolling pin or a pasta machine, roll the pasta dough into very thin sheets. Let the sheets dry briefly. Cut into strips 1½ inches wide.

Place portions of the filling, about 1 teaspoon each, about 1 inch apart on one of the strips. Brush the beaten egg onto the strip between the portions of filling. Place another strip on top and press down with your fingers all around the filling to expel any air and seal the two strips together. Cut between filling portions with a knife or a pastry wheel. Press the edges together again to seal and set aside. Repeat with the remaining dough and filling.

Bring a large pot of salted water to a boil and cook the pasta until it floats to the surface. [Fresh egg pasta cooks quickly.]

Meanwhile, melt the butter in a large skillet. Add the sage leaves and sauté until crispy, about 3 minutes.

Drain the pasta when cooked (you may want to use a skimmer rather than overturning the pot into a colander as the pasta is delicate) and transfer the pasta to a large serving bowl. Pour the melted butter with the sage leaves over the ravioli and toss gently to combine. Season with additional black pepper and the remaining 1 cup Parmigiano.

HOW TO MAKE GNOCCHI

1 Drain the cooked potatoes, and when they are cool enough to handle, peel them.

2 Spread riced potatoes on the work surface.

3 Mix in the egg yolks and toss to combine.

4 Knead in the flour and continue kneading into a smooth dough.

5 Roll the dough into large cylinders.

6 Don't worry about making these large cylinders perfectly smooth.

7 Cut the large cylinders into smaller chunks, each about the size of an egg.

8 Using your hands, on a lightly floured surface roll each piece of dough into a smaller cylinder about as thick as your thumb.

9 Cut the narrow cylinders into ¾-inch lengths with a knife or bench scraper.

10 As you cut the gnocchi, transfer them to a lightly floured baking sheet and toss with a little extra flour. Spread them in a single layer.

GNOCCHI AL GORGONZOLA

The town of Gorgonzola in Lombardy is famed for its flavorful cheese made of cow's milk and threaded with blue or green veins. Gorgonzola may be rather mild or so sharp that it is almost spicy. It melts into a creamy sauce for gnocchi.

SERVES 4

4 medium russet potatoes

3 egg yolks

1½ cups unbleached all-purpose flour, plus more for dusting

Salt to taste

3 cups heavy cream

5 to 6 ounces mild gorgonzola

½ cup chopped walnuts

¼ cup minced parsley

1 cup grated Parmigiano Reggiano

Bring a large pot of water to a boil and boil the potatoes until they are tender enough to pierce easily with a paring knife. Don't check too often, as cutting through the skin may cause them to grow waterlogged. Drain the cooked potatoes, and when they are cool enough to handle, peel them and crush them with a potato ricer, letting them fall into a bowl. Let the potatoes cool to room temperature.

Add the egg yolks to the potatoes and stir to combine, then add the 1½ cups flour. Knead by hand in the bowl until the ingredients are well combined. Lightly flour the work surface and transfer every last bit of dough from the bowl to the surface. Continue to knead, adding flour in very small amounts (but cautiously, as it is easy to make the dough too heavy), until the dough is soft and still slightly tacky, but not so sticky that it sticks to your fingers. Clean the work surface, lightly flour it, and divide the dough into 6 to 8 equal pieces. With the palms of your hands, roll each piece of dough into a cylinder as thick as your thumb. Cut the cylinders into pieces roughly ¾ inch long. As you finish them, set them aside on a lightly floured surface and dust very lightly with flour.

Bring a large pot of salted water to a boil and cook the gnocchi in batches until they float to the surface. At the same time, place the cream and gorgonzola in a saucepan and place over low heat, stirring occasionally. As the gnocchi are cooked, remove them with a slotted spoon or skimmer. When all the gnocchi are cooked, transfer them to the saucepan and cook, tossing gently, over high heat for 1 minute. Divide the pasta among individual serving bowls and top with the walnuts, parsley, and the grated Parmigiano.

RISOTTO WITH ASPARAGUS

Technically rice is a grain, not a kind of pasta, but risotto is a first course in Italy akin to a pasta dish. Risotto is prepared by adding broth little by little to cook arborio rice so that it slowly forms its own creamy sauce. Once you learn the technique for making risotto, the possibilities are limitless. All you really need is a healthy stirring arm.

SERVES 4

5 pounds beef or chicken bones

2 carrots

2 small yellow onions

2 ribs celery

1 sprig parsley

3 tablespoons extra-virgin olive oil

1½ cups arborio rice

½ cup white wine

**1 pound asparagus, cut into 2-inch
    lengths**

1 cup grated Parmigiano Reggiano

1 tablespoon unsalted butter

Salt to taste

Freshly ground black pepper to taste

Place the bones in a stockpot. Add the carrots, 1 onion, the celery, and parsley. Add water to cover. Bring to a boil, then cover with a tight-fitting lid and reduce the heat to a gentle simmer. Simmer for 3 to 4 hours, occasionally removing foam with a skimmer. Add hot water to keep ingredients submerged, if needed. When the broth is ready, strain it through a cheesecloth-lined colander or strainer, then return it to the pot. Bring to a simmer over low heat.

Chop the 1 remaining onion and heat the olive oil in a large skillet or saucepan. Sauté the chopped onion for 2 minutes, then add the rice. Sauté, stirring constantly, for 2 additional minutes, then add the wine. Continue to cook, stirring frequently, and when the wine has been absorbed by the rice, add about ½ cup of the warm stock to the saucepan. Simmer, stirring constantly, until most of the broth has been absorbed, then add another ½ cup of broth. Continue stirring and adding stock when the previous addition has been absorbed, decreasing the amount added slightly each time. After about 10 minutes add the asparagus and continue cooking. When the rice is al dente, about 10 additional minutes, remove it from the heat. Stir in the Parmigiano and the butter, season to taste with salt and black pepper, and stir vigorously to combine.

CHAPTER 4

MAIN COURSES

OUTSIDE OF ITALY, THE COUNTRY'S *SECONDI*, or main courses, are often less well known than its *primi* (first courses of pasta, rice, and soup), and that's unfair. With its many miles of coastline along the Mediterranean and the Adriatic, Italy has plentiful fish options that make satisfying second courses, while the North's green valleys and the slopes of the Apennines offer an ideal environment for cattle farming.

This wealth of varied food sources is nothing new: genetic analysis of bones, frescoes in Pompeii and elsewhere, and period writings show that two thousand years ago the peninsula's inhabitants already ate ox, sheep, goat, pig, deer, boar, hare, and other meats. They enjoyed many varieties of fish and seafood, including anchovies, grouper, sardines, eel, and lobster. Today as then, these items tend to be prepared simply and in ways that enhance their natural qualities. Many of these main courses incorporate vegetables; for any that don't, choose one or two side dishes from Chapter 5 as an accompaniment.

SEARED SALMON WITH FARRO

Farro is one of the oldest cultivated grains and was a staple food of the Roman legions. Today, farro is grown in Lazio, Tuscany, and the Marche—and Umbria is home to DOP farro from Monteleone di Spoleto.

SERVES 4

1½ cups farro, rinsed and drained

¼ cup plus 1 tablespoon extra-virgin olive oil

1 pound salmon fillet

Salt to taste

Freshly ground black pepper to taste

1 sprig dill, chopped

Place 4 cups water in a large pot and bring to a boil. Add the farro, reduce the heat to low, and cook, covered, until the farro is tender, 25 to 30 minutes. Drain if needed (the farro may absorb all of the water or there may be some left in the bottom of the pot).

Heat 2 tablespoons olive oil in a large skillet and place over medium heat. Add the drained farro and sauté for 3 minutes.

In a clean skillet, heat the remaining 3 tablespoons olive oil and sear the salmon for 2 minutes per side. Arrange the salmon on top of the farro. Season to taste with salt and black pepper and scatter on the dill.

GRILLED TUNA DEL PRINCIPE

Tuna fishing is a centuries-old Sicilian tradition, and the cooks of the island know the best way to highlight fresh tuna is to treat it simply and allow its natural goodness to come to the fore. This dish is named after the scion of a noble Italian house, the Prince Pignatelli della Leonessa, whose family was originally from Naples.

SERVES 4

¼ cup plus 2 tablespoons extra-virgin olive oil

1 zucchini, chopped

2 yellow squash, chopped

1 orange bell pepper, cored, seeded, and chopped

1 red bell pepper, cored, seeded, and chopped

Salt to taste

Freshly ground black pepper to taste

1¾ pounds fresh tuna

Heat ¼ cup olive oil in a skillet and sauté the vegetables until soft, 7 to 8 minutes. Season to taste with salt and black pepper.

Meanwhile, preheat a charcoal or gas grill to high heat. Season the tuna on both sides with salt and black pepper and brush the grill with the remaining 2 tablespoons olive oil. Place the tuna on the grill and cook without moving it until the bottom has grill marks but the center remains very rare. Turn 45 degrees to make a grid of grill marks, then flip and grill the other side. Let the tuna rest for about 5 minutes before slicing. Serve with vegetables.

CHICKEN PAILLARD

A paillard is a boneless piece of meat or chicken pounded thin. It is delicious grilled or browned in a pan. Either way, it cooks very quickly. The paillard is named after the proprietor of the eponymous Restaurant Paillard, a celebrated Parisian eatery in the 1890s.

SERVES 4

2 cups baby arugula

¼ cup extra-virgin olive oil

Salt to taste

Freshly ground black pepper to taste

2 chicken breasts

10 cherry tomatoes, halved

Dress the arugula with the olive oil, salt, and black pepper, toss to combine, then set aside.

Cut the chicken breasts in half so you have 4 pieces and evenly pound them very thin using a meat mallet. Preheat a charcoal or gas grill to medium. Brush oil on the grill, then cook the chicken until opaque and marked with grill marks, turning once.

Place the chicken on a platter. Mound the arugula salad in the middle and garnish with the cherry tomatoes.

ROASTED CORNISH GAME HEN

Rosemary, a perennial herb that is native to the Mediterranean, adds a distinctive accent to poultry. Ancient Romans used rosemary both as an herb and as medicine. Little Cornish game hens are so visually appealing that it's nice to put everything together in the baking pan and serve this at the table.

SERVES 4

¼ cup plus 1 tablespoon extra-virgin olive oil

2 Cornish game hens

2 lemons

Leaves of 1 sprig rosemary

1 pound red potatoes, cut into wedges

1 pound baby spinach

Salt to taste

Freshly ground black pepper to taste

Preheat the oven to 375°F.

Rub 2 tablespoons olive oil all over the hens and put a lemon in the cavity of each hen. Place in a large baking pan, scatter on the rosemary, and roast for 30 minutes.

Meanwhile, place 3 tablespoons olive oil in a skillet over medium-high heat. Sauté the potatoes for 5 minutes, then remove from the heat. When the hens have been in the oven for 30 minutes, add the potatoes to the baking pan. Continue roasting until the potatoes are browned and the flesh of the hens is opaque, about 1 hour total for the hens.

Bring a pot of water to a boil and cook the spinach for 1 minute. Drain, squeeze dry, and set aside.

When the hens are ready, remove the pan from oven and add the spinach. Season with salt and black pepper.

VEAL MILANESE

A thin, crisp cotoletta sits on the list of Milanese classics alongside saffron risotto, osso buco, and Christmas panettone. In 1783, at the height of the rivalry between Milan, at the time one of the richest cities in the Austrian empire, and Vienna, Milanese Pietro Verri published a history of Milan that claimed Milan had invented the breaded veal cutlet in the twelfth century and implying that the Wiener schnitzel was a pallid imitation. Traditionally veal Milanese is made with a bone-in chop. A butcher may even pound the chops thin for you. Some people like a spritz of lemon atop this dish, and others prefer a scattering of chopped tomatoes.

SERVES 4

4 large eggs

¼ cup whole milk

Salt to taste

Freshly ground black pepper to taste

2 cups dry breadcrumbs

4 bone-in veal chops, pounded very thin

Olive oil for frying

In a shallow bowl, whisk the eggs with the milk, salt, and black pepper. Place the breadcrumbs in a separate shallow bowl. Dip 1 chop in the beaten egg, then dredge in the breadcrumbs until fully coated. Set aside and repeat with the remaining chops, arranging them in a single layer on a platter or baking sheet.

Place several inches of oil for frying in a large skillet with high sides and heat the oil to 375°F. Line a baking sheet with paper towels and set aside. Working in batches if necessary to keep from crowding the skillet, fry the chops in the oil, turning once, until golden and crisp. (If you are working in batches, wait for the oil to return to 375˚F before frying the next batch.) Remove from the oil with a slotted spatula and place on the prepared pan to drain briefly.

LA FIORENTINA

The pride of Florence, this is a thick and juicy T-bone or porterhouse from the loin of a Chianina cow. The Chianina breed has been raised in Tuscany, as well as Umbria and Lazio, for at least two thousand two hundred years.

SERVES 4

1 porterhouse or T-bone steak, preferably Chianina beef, 2 to 3 inches thick

Salt to taste

Freshly ground black pepper to taste

1 tablespoon extra-virgin olive oil

1 sprig rosemary

Preheat a gas or charcoal grill to high. Rub the meat with a mixture of salt and black pepper. Brush the grill with the olive oil and place the steak on the grill. Grill the steak for 5 minutes without moving it, then turn it and grill it for another 5 minutes. Turn the steak again and grill for 4 minutes on the first side, finally turn it one more time and grill for an additional 4 minutes. If you prefer your meat more well done, continue to grill until desired doneness. Remove the meat from the grill and place it on a cutting board with the rosemary on top. Let it rest for 5 minutes. Serve whole or sliced.

GRILLED FILET MIGNON WITH CRISTINA'S SEASONED SALT

Filet mignon is a tender cut of beef that is so luxurious to begin with that it requires only the simplest cooking methods. In Italy we often sprinkle meat with sale profumato, made by combining salt with spices. Cristina Rizzo, a dear friend of Vittorio and Fabio, is a master of the technique and contributed this recipe.

SERVES 4

Coarse salt to taste

Coarsely ground black pepper to taste

Coarsely ground pink pepper to taste

Dried rosemary to taste

Dried sage to taste

2 filet mignon, about 11 ounces each

Olive oil for brushing

2 sprigs rosemary for garnish

Make a mixture of salt, both types of pepper, and crumbled rosemary and sage. Preheat a gas or charcoal grill to high heat. Rub the meat with the salt mixture. Brush the grill with olive oil and place the steaks on the grill. Cook to desired doneness. Cooking time will depend on thickness, but typically it will take 5 to 6 minutes per side to reach medium-rare. Remove the steaks from the grill and allow them to rest for 5 minutes. Slice and transfer to a serving platter. Garnish with rosemary.

STUFATO DI MANZO

Stufato di manzo is a long-cooked beef stew—the ultimate winter comfort food. *Stufato* derives from the Italian word for stove, as this dish was traditionally cooked on top of a stove that did double duty, as it was used both for heating the home and for cooking. Serve with plenty of mashed or roasted potatoes.

SERVES 4

2 to 3 tablespoons extra-virgin olive oil

1 pound beef chuck or other stew meat

½ cup white or red wine

1 15-ounce can whole peeled tomatoes

1 tablespoon dried oregano

1 sprig rosemary

Salt to taste

Freshly ground black pepper to taste

½ teaspoon crushed red pepper

Place the olive oil in a large pot and place over high heat. Sear the meat until browned on all sides. Add the wine, tomatoes, oregano, rosemary, salt, black pepper, and crushed red pepper. Cover and reduce heat to low. Simmer, stirring occasionally, until the meat is soft enough to shred with a fork and the tomatoes have broken down, at least 1 hour. Remove and discard rosemary sprig before serving.

BRAISED LENTILS, ROASTED POTATOES & BRUSSELS SPROUTS

Lentils are possibly the oldest cultivated legume in the world with a historical record as a food source that goes back seven thousand years in the Near East and Turkey. The lentils from Italy's Umbria region, like the tiny and delicate Castelluccio di Norcia IGP lentils, are fantastic and you should seek them out. Lentils are eaten frequently year-round in Italy, but they are a must on New Year's Eve, when they are thought to bring good luck in the coming year.

SERVES 4

3 to 4 new potatoes, peeled and quartered

Extra-virgin olive oil for brushing, dressing, and sautéing

1 clove garlic, minced

Leaves of 1 sprig rosemary

Salt to taste

Freshly ground black pepper to taste

1 cup dried lentils, rinsed and drained

7 to 8 Brussels sprouts

Preheat the oven to 350°F. Brush the potatoes with oil and toss them with the garlic and rosemary. Season with salt and black pepper. Spread the potatoes in a single layer in a pan and bake, turning occasionally, until easily pierced with a paring knife and browned and crisp on the outside, 30 to 40 minutes.

Meanwhile, in a large pot, combine the lentils with 2 cups water. Bring to a boil, then reduce the heat and simmer uncovered until tender, about 30 minutes. Drain and dress with olive oil, salt, and black pepper or according to taste.

Bring a large pot of water to a boil. Boil the Brussels sprouts until tender, 3 to 4 minutes. Drain, core, and cut in half. In a skillet, heat a generous amount of olive oil and sauté the Brussels sprouts until browned, about 8 minutes. Season with salt and black pepper.

Serve the vegetables separately.

POLENTA

Polenta is from Northern Italy: a kind of porridge made with coarsely ground cornmeal that is known as *cucina povera* because its ingredients were inexpensive and readily available. Discriminating cooks love polenta for its versatility and subtle flavor. Yellow corn polenta is the most common type, but there is also a white variety available. Polenta is delicious with braised meats and stews.

SERVES 4

1 cup cornmeal for polenta
¼ teaspoon salt

In a large pot, bring 4 cups water to a boil. Let the polenta fall into the pot in a thin stream between your fingers, almost grain by grain, while whisking constantly. When you have added all the polenta, whisk vigorously and ensure that there are no lumps. Reduce the heat to low and simmer, whisking frequently, until the polenta starts to thicken, about 5 minutes. Switch to a wooden spoon and cook, stirring constantly, until the polenta is creamy and no longer tastes raw, about 30 additional minutes.

CIPOLLINE DOLCI

Cipollini onions (*cipolline* in Italian) are squat little bulbs with a flat top. They are small enough to be cooked and served whole, and sweet enough to take center stage in their own dish rather than playing a supporting role as onions so often do. These make a tasty foil for roasted meat.

SERVES 4

1 pound cipollini onions, peeled

2 tablespoons unsalted butter

½ cup sugar

1 tablespoon white balsamic vinegar

Bring a large pot of water to a boil and cook the cipollini for 5 minutes. Drain and set aside.

In a large saucepan, combine the butter, sugar, and vinegar with 1 cup water and place over medium-low heat until the butter has melted and the sugar has dissolved. Stir to combine, then add the cipollini and stir to coat them. Cover and cook over medium-low heat, stirring frequently and adding water in small amounts if the pan starts to get dry, until the onions are tender enough to pierce with a paring knife but still hold their shape, about 10 minutes.

ASPARAGUS WITH ROASTED POTATOES & PARMIGIANO REGGIANO

Slender or fat, wild or cultivated, green or white—the asparagus heralds the Italian spring.

SERVES 4

3 to 4 new potatoes, peeled and
    quartered

Extra-virgin olive oil for brushing and
    sautéing

1 clove garlic, minced

Leaves of 1 sprig rosemary

Salt to taste

Freshly ground black pepper to taste

1 bunch asparagus, trimmed

½ cup grated Parmigiano Reggiano

Preheat the oven to 350°F. Brush the potatoes with oil and toss them with the garlic and rosemary. Season with salt and black pepper. Spread the potatoes in a single layer on a baking sheet and bake, turning occasionally, until easily pierced with a paring knife and browned and crisp on the outside, 30 to 40 minutes.

Meanwhile, bring a large pot of salted water to a boil.

Cook the asparagus in the boiling water for 5 minutes, then drain. Heat a generous amount of olive oil in a skillet. Sauté the asparagus for few minutes. Remove the asparagus from the heat and sprinkle the grated Parmigiano on top.

CHAPTER 6

PIZZA

PIZZA IS A MEAL UNTO ITSELF and one that has evolved over centuries, traveling far from its origin as a Roman soldier's ration to become a humble street food in Naples and, finally, to achieve its current ubiquitous global standing. The great transformative moment in Neapolitan pizza occurred in the 1700s, when tomato was added to what had previously been a round of dough topped with cheese. (The term pizza is ancient and appears in the 997 AD tome *Codex Diplomaticus Caietanus* discovered in the Abbey of Montecassino, near Gaeta.)

The European Union recently recognized Neapolitan pizza cooked in a wood-burning oven as a Traditional Guaranteed Specialty (STG) product with three officially recognized variations: pizza marinara topped with tomatoes, garlic, oregano, and extra-virgin olive oil; pizza margherita, which also features mozzarella and basil; and pizza extra with mozzarella di bufala. To meet STG requirements, the dough must be made with Italian type 0 or 00 flour, fresh yeast, water, and salt. Serafina imports highly refined 00 flour that is produced especially for them by Molini Pivetti to all its locations. The flour is milled from non-GMO wheat harvested only in Pivetti's certified fields. It actually goes beyond STG requirements, and it makes a highly digestible—not to mention delicious—pizza dough.

But while standards may be strict for official Neapolitan pizza, generally pizza preferences are quite personal, and everyone, from Tokyo to Los Angeles, from London to Dubai, and from Sao Paolo to Miami has a favorite. We are sure you will find a few you love in this chapter.

PIZZA ROSSA CON OLIVE

———

Italians call a pizza with tomato but no mozzarella a *pizza rossa*, or red pizza. San Marzano tomatoes that grow around Naples are traditionally used on pizza, but any variety will work, as long as the tomatoes are fully ripened. There's no need to cook the tomatoes in advance—the hot oven takes care of that.

MAKES TWO 10-INCH PIZZAS

1 15-ounce can whole peeled tomatoes

2 tablespoons extra-virgin olive oil

Salt to taste

Freshly ground black pepper to taste

2 crusts for 10-inch pizzas [page 231]

30 black olives

¼ cup grated Parmigiano Reggiano

2 sprigs rosemary

Dried oregano to taste

Preheat the oven, with a baking stone in it if you have one, to 475°F for at least 30 minutes.

Crush the tomatoes and their liquid through a potato ricer, letting them drop into a bowl. Stir in the olive oil and season with salt and black pepper. Spread equal amounts of the tomato mixture onto the pizza crusts, leaving the perimeters bare, then scatter on the olives.

Place the pizzas in the preheated oven (or slide them onto the baking stone, if using) and bake until the crusts are golden, 10 to 15 minutes. Remove from the oven, sprinkle with grated cheese, and garnish each with a rosemary sprig. Scatter on a little oregano.

PIZZA MARGHERITA

Another official type of Neapolitan pizza, a pizza margherita is topped with tomato sauce, mozzarella, basil, and extra-virgin olive oil. You can play on the classic with black olives, as we do here, or thinly sliced mushrooms or other toppings.

MAKES TWO 10-INCH PIZZAS

1 15-ounce can whole peeled tomatoes

2 tablespoons extra-virgin olive oil

Salt to taste

Freshly ground black pepper to taste

2 crusts for 10-inch pizzas (page 231)

6 ounces mozzarella, drained

¼ cup black olives, pitted

Basil leaves for garnish

Preheat the oven, with a baking stone in it if you have one, to 475°F for at least 30 minutes.

Crush the tomatoes and their liquid through a potato ricer, letting them drop into a bowl. Stir in the olive oil and season with salt and black pepper. Spread equal amounts of the tomato mixture onto the pizza crusts, leaving the perimeters bare. Slice the mozzarella and arrange it in a single layer on the pizzas. Scatter on the olives.

Place the pizzas in the preheated oven (or slide them onto the baking stone, if using) and bake until the crusts are golden, 10 to 15 minutes. Remove from the oven and garnish with basil.

REGINA MARGHERITA PIZZA

When Margherita of Savoy was crowned queen, or *regina*, she is said to have come through Naples on a tour of her kingdom and inquired about the food she saw so many of her new subjects eating—a mysterious dish known as pizza. That's the legend, but despite the fact that she was a very popular queen, many Neapolitans reject the idea that the pizza margherita was named for her and instead say it was named for a daisy, a *margherita* in Italian, because the slices of mozzarella are arranged like the petals of the flower.

MAKES TWO 10-INCH PIZZAS

1 15-ounce can whole peeled tomatoes

2 tablespoons extra-virgin olive oil

Salt to taste

Freshly ground black pepper to taste

2 crusts for 10-inch pizzas [page 231]

8 ounces mozzarella, drained

10 cherry tomatoes, halved

½ cup grated Parmigiano Reggiano

Basil leaves for garnish

Preheat the oven, with a baking stone in it if you have one, to 475°F for at least 30 minutes.

Crush the tomatoes and their liquid through a potato ricer, letting them drop into a bowl. Stir in the olive oil and season with salt and black pepper. Spread equal amounts of the tomato mixture onto the pizza dough, leaving the perimeters bare. Slice the mozzarella and arrange it in a single layer on the pizzas. Scatter on the halved cherry tomatoes, then sprinkle on the Parmigiano.

Place the pizzas in the preheated oven (or slide them onto the baking stone, if using) and bake until the crusts are golden, 10 to 15 minutes. Remove from the oven and garnish with basil.

PIZZA VIP MARGHERITA WITH FIOR DI LATTE

Pizza is sometimes made with mozzarella di bufala from Campania, in the areas around Caserta and Naples. This prized cheese is made from the milk of black water buffalo introduced to the southern Italian marshlands centuries ago. Cow's milk mozzarella is known as fior di latte. It is creamier than the buffalo milk type. Mountain breeds, such as Agnone and Bojano in Alto Molise, provide the best milk for this type of mozzarella. Try both and see which one you like better—it's really a matter of taste.

MAKES TWO 10-INCH PIZZAS

1 15-ounce can whole peeled tomatoes
2 tablespoons extra-virgin olive oil
Salt to taste
Freshly ground black pepper to taste
2 crusts for 10-inch pizzas [page 231]
6 ounces fior di latte mozzarella, drained
10 cherry tomatoes, halved
½ cup grated Parmigiano Reggiano
Basil leaves for garnish

Preheat the oven, with a baking stone in it if you have one, to 475°F for at least 30 minutes.

Crush the tomatoes and their liquid through a potato ricer, letting them drop into a bowl. Stir in the olive oil and season with salt and black pepper. Spread equal amounts of the tomato mixture onto the pizza dough, leaving the perimeters bare. Slice the mozzarella and arrange it in a single layer on the pizzas. Scatter on the halved cherry tomatoes, then sprinkle on the Parmigiano.

Place the pizzas in the preheated oven (or slide them onto the baking stone, if using) and bake until the crusts are golden, 10 to 15 minutes. Remove from the oven and garnish with basil.

PIZZA QUATTRO STAGIONI

This pizza represents the four seasons: mushrooms for fall; prosciutto for winter; artichokes for spring; and pesto for summer. Rather than being scattered on the pizza together, each is kept in its own quadrant.

MAKES TWO 10-INCH PIZZAS

2 to 3 baby artichokes

2 cloves garlic

Leaves of 1 sprig parsley, minced

5 cups basil leaves

1½ cups pine nuts

¼ cup plus 3 tablespoons extra-virgin olive oil

Salt to taste

2 ounces Parmigiano Reggiano

1 15-ounce can whole peeled tomatoes

Freshly ground black pepper to taste

2 crusts for 10-inch pizzas (page 231)

6 ounces mozzarella, drained

1 cup sliced shiitake mushrooms

4 ounces thinly sliced prosciutto di Parma

¼ cup Parmigiano Reggiano shavings

½ cup tightly packed baby arugula

Preheat the oven, with a baking stone in it if you have one, to 475°F for at least 30 minutes.

Prepare the artichokes by removing the outer leaves and then cut them into small pieces. Mince 1 clove garlic. Add the artichokes, minced garlic, and parsley to a small skillet and add 1 to 2 tablespoons of water. Cook over medium heat until tender, about 8 minutes. Add water a little at a time if necessary to keep the artichokes from sticking to the pan. Set aside.

In a blender combine the basil, pine nuts, remaining clove garlic, ¼ cup plus 1 tablespoon olive oil, and a pinch of salt. Blend until smooth, with only a few green flecks left. Then add the 2 ounces Parmigiano and blend until thick.

Crush the tomatoes and their liquid through a potato ricer, letting them drop into a bowl. Stir in the remaining 2 tablespoons olive oil and season with salt and black pepper. Spread equal amounts of the tomato mixture onto the pizza dough, leaving the perimeters bare.

Dice the mozzarella and scatter it evenly over the tomato sauce on both pizzas. Arrange the sliced mushrooms on one quarter of each pizza and the artichokes on a second quarter. Leave half of each pizza without toppings.

Place the pizzas in the preheated oven (or slide them onto the baking stone, if using) and bake until the crusts are golden, 10 to 15 minutes. Remove from the oven and arrange the prosciutto on one quarter of each and drizzle the pesto on the remaining quarter. Scatter the Parmigiano shavings over the entire pizzas. Mound half of the arugula in the center of each pizza. Or you can always vary how you place the ingredients; here the arugula is on one quarter and we have combined the pesto and artichokes—uniting spring and summer.

PIZZA ALLA NORCINA

Norcia (Norcina is the adjective) is a town in Umbria known for its pork products and especially its sausage, which marries well with the abundant mushrooms found locally. Sometimes a pizza with mushrooms is known as a boscaiola pizza, a reference to woodcutters who often stumbled upon delicious mushrooms when working in the forest.

MAKES TWO 10-INCH PIZZAS

1 cup sliced shiitake mushrooms

3 tablespoons extra-virgin olive oil

½ cup white wine

Salt to taste

Freshly ground black pepper to taste

1 link hot Italian pork sausage

1 15-ounce can whole peeled tomatoes

2 crusts for 10-inch pizzas [page 231]

6 ounces mozzarella, drained and sliced

Crushed red pepper to taste

Basil leaves for garnish

Preheat the oven, with a baking stone in it if you have one, to 475°F for at least 30 minutes.

In a skillet, sauté the mushrooms in 1 tablespoon olive oil. Add the wine and cook until evaporated, then season with salt and black pepper and cook until tender. Remove from the heat. Remove the casing from the sausage and crumble it into a small bowl. Toss with the cooked mushrooms and set aside.

Crush the tomatoes and their liquid through a potato ricer, letting them drop into a bowl. Stir in the remaining 2 tablespoons olive oil and season with salt and black pepper. Spread equal amounts of the tomato mixture onto the pizza dough, leaving the perimeters bare. Place the mozzarella on top of the tomato sauce and scatter the mushroom and sausage mixture on top.

Place the pizzas in the preheated oven [or slide them onto the baking stone, if using] and bake until the crusts are golden, 10 to 15 minutes. Remove from the oven, season with crushed red pepper, and garnish with basil.

PIZZA ALL'UOVO

A pizza with an egg cooked on top is sometimes known as pizza alla Bismarck, in
reference to nineteenth-century German chancellor Otto von Bismarck, who was said
to be able to eat as many as twelve eggs in one sitting.

MAKES TWO 10-INCH PIZZAS

1 15-ounce can whole peeled tomatoes

2 tablespoons extra-virgin olive oil

Salt to taste

Freshly ground black pepper to taste

2 crusts for 10-inch pizzas (page 231)

6 ounces mozzarella, drained and sliced

2 large eggs

4 ounces thinly sliced prosciutto di Parma

Crushed red pepper to taste

Preheat the oven, with a baking stone in it if you have one, to 475°F for at least 30 minutes.

Crush the tomatoes and their liquid through a potato ricer, letting them drop into a bowl. Stir in the olive oil and season with salt and black pepper. Spread equal amounts of the tomato mixture onto the pizza dough, leaving the perimeters bare. Arrange mozzarella evenly on the tomato sauce.

Place the pizzas in the preheated oven (or slide them onto the baking stone, if using) and bake until the crusts are golden, but not quite browned, 8 to 12 minutes. Remove the pizzas from the oven and top each with an egg. Return to the oven and bake until the crusts are fully browned but the egg yolks are still soft. Remove from the oven and arrange the prosciutto on the pizzas. Season with crushed red pepper.

PIZZA PRIMAVERA

Vincenzo Corrado, the famous Neapolitan cook and author of the 1773 bestseller *Il cuoco galante*, also wrote a treatise on the culinary habits of Neapolitans. In that text he observed people were using newfangled imported tomatoes on both pasta and pizza. The latter he described as a thin disk of dough flavored with lard, tomato, and herbs. This account is said to be the first published mention of pizza.

MAKES TWO 10-INCH PIZZAS

1 cup sliced button mushrooms

3 tablespoons extra-virgin olive oil

½ cup white wine

Salt to taste

Freshly ground black pepper to taste

2 to 3 baby artichokes

1 clove garlic, minced

½ cup chopped parsley

1 15-ounce can whole peeled tomatoes

2 crusts for 10-inch pizzas (page 231)

6 ounces mozzarella, drained and sliced

2 to 3 small zucchini, thinly sliced

½ cup pitted black olives

Preheat the oven, with a baking stone in it if you have one, to 475°F for at least 30 minutes.

In a skillet, sauté the mushrooms in 1 tablespoon olive oil. Add the wine and cook until evaporated, then season with salt and black pepper and cook until tender. Remove from the heat.

Prepare the artichokes by removing the outer leaves. Slice into quarters and then slice thinly. Add the artichokes, minced garlic, and parsley to a small skillet and add 1 to 2 tablespoons of water. Cook over medium heat until tender, about 8 minutes. Add water a little at a time if necessary to keep the artichokes from sticking to the pan. Set aside.

Crush the tomatoes and their liquid through a potato ricer, letting them drop into a bowl. Stir in the remaining 2 tablespoons olive oil and season with salt and black pepper. Spread equal amounts of the tomato mixture onto the pizza dough, leaving the perimeters bare, then arrange the mozzarella on top of the tomato sauce. Scatter the vegetables and the olives evenly over the two pizzas.

Place the pizzas in the preheated oven (or slide them onto the baking stone, if using) and bake until the crusts are golden, 10 to 15 minutes.

PIZZA BIANCA VEGETARIANA

This pizza is a longtime spring favorite and pleases vegetarians and carnivores alike. Holding back the Parmigiano and adding it at the end on top of the melted cheese provides an interesting contrast.

MAKES TWO 10-INCH PIZZAS

5 ounces mozzarella, drained and sliced

2 crusts for 10-inch pizzas [page 231]

5 ounces fontina cheese, sliced

2 cups baby arugula

1 cup Parmigiano Reggiano shavings

Crushed red pepper to taste

Preheat the oven, with a baking stone in it if you have one, to 475°F for at least 30 minutes.

Arrange the mozzarella on the two crusts, leaving the perimeters bare. Arrange the fontina on top of the mozzarella.

Place the pizzas in the preheated oven [or slide them onto the baking stone, if using] and bake until the crusts are golden, 10 to 15 minutes. Remove from the oven, mound half of the arugula in the center of each pizza, and top with the Parmigiano shavings and crushed red pepper.

EGGPLANT & GOAT CHEESE PIZZA

Eggplant is a staple of Southern Italian cooking and appears in a variety of traditional dishes. Eggplant is actually a fruit, though it is treated as a vegetable. It earned its name in the middle of the eighteenth century, as the variety most widely known at the time resembled an egg.

MAKES TWO 10-INCH PIZZAS

1 eggplant, thinly sliced

¼ cup extra-virgin olive oil

6 ounces mozzarella, drained and sliced

2 crusts for 10-inch pizzas (page 231)

6 ounces goat cheese

10 cherry tomatoes, halved

Crushed red pepper to taste

2 cups baby arugula

Preheat the oven, with a baking stone in it if you have one, to 475°F for at least 30 minutes.

Preheat a charcoal or gas grill to medium-high heat. Brush the eggplant slices with olive oil and grill them until grill marks appear on one side. Turn and continue cooking until grill marks appear on the other side and the slices are soft.

Arrange the mozzarella on the two crusts, leaving the perimeters bare. Crumble the goat cheese and scatter it on as well, then top with the eggplant slices and the halved tomatoes.

Place the pizzas in the preheated oven (or slide them onto the baking stone, if using) and bake until the crusts are golden, 10 to 15 minutes. Remove from the oven, season with crushed red pepper, then mound half of the arugula in the center of each pizza.

PIZZA DI VITTORIO

Vittorio Assaf prefers his pizza prepared with classic ingredients topped with creamy burrata from Puglia. Burrata consists of an outer pouch of more solid cheese filled with softer cheese inside, and it offers a rich and luscious texture that counterbalances the earthiness of the tomato.

MAKES TWO 10-INCH PIZZAS

1 15-ounce can whole peeled tomatoes

2 tablespoons extra-virgin olive oil

Salt to taste

Freshly ground black pepper to taste

2 crusts for 10-inch pizzas [page 231]

6 ounces burrata, shredded by hand

Basil leaves for garnish

Preheat the oven, with a baking stone in it if you have one, to 475°F for at least 30 minutes.

Crush the tomatoes and their liquid through a potato ricer, letting them drop into a bowl. Stir in the 2 tablespoons olive oil and season with salt and black pepper. Spread equal amounts of the tomato mixture onto the pizza crusts, leaving the perimeters bare.

Place the pizzas in the preheated oven (or slide them onto the baking stone, if using) and bake until the crusts are golden, 10 to 15 minutes. Remove from the oven.

Shred the burrata by hand and arrange it on the hot pizzas. This will allow the burrata to melt from the heat of the pizza without cooking it. Garnish with basil.

A twist to this pizza recipe includes placing a slice of thin prosciutto di Parma on each quarter just before serving.

PIZZA ALLA BRESAOLA

The combination of bresaola and arugula is a perennial favorite in the Lombardy region. A "bianca" or "white" pizza, i.e., one without tomato sauce, serves as a blank canvas that really showcases the flavors.

MAKES TWO 10-INCH PIZZAS

6 ounces mozzarella, drained and sliced

2 ounces Fontina cheese, sliced

2 crusts for 10-inch pizzas (page 231)

2 cups baby arugula or watercress

2 tablespoons extra-virgin olive oil

¼ teaspoon grated Parmigiano Reggiano

Crushed red pepper to taste

4 ounces thinly sliced bresaola

Preheat the oven, with a baking stone in it if you have one, to 475°F for at least 30 minutes.

Arrange the mozzarella and the Fontina cheese on the two crusts, leaving the perimeters bare.

Place the pizzas in the preheated oven (or slide them onto the baking stone, if using) and bake until the crusts are golden, 10 to 15 minutes.

While the pizza is cooking, put the arugula in a mixing bowl. Add a touch of oil and the Parmigiano and toss. You can also add crushed red pepper if you wish.

Remove from the oven, place the bresaola in a single layer on both pizzas, then mound half of the arugula in the center of each pizza.

PIZZA WITH PROSCIUTTO & FIGS

Prosciutto and figs are a classic combination and a summer staple in Italy. Fresh, ripe figs are a must. Their sweet flavor plays off of the salt of the prosciutto perfectly.

MAKES TWO 10-INCH PIZZAS

1 cup heavy cream

¾ cup grated Parmigiano Reggiano

2 crusts for 10-inch pizzas (page 231)

4 to 6 fresh figs, halved

5 ounces thinly sliced prosciutto di Parma

Basil leaves for garnish

Preheat the oven, with a baking stone in it if you have one, to 475°F for at least 30 minutes.

Place the cream in a saucepan and bring to a simmer over medium heat. Simmer until reduced, about 5 minutes, then stir in the Parmigiano and whisk to combine. Spread this mixture over the crusts, leaving the perimeters bare. Arrange the fig halves cut sides up on the cream topping.

Place the pizzas in the preheated oven (or slide them onto the baking stone, if using) and bake until the crusts are golden, 10 to 15 minutes. Remove from the oven and arrange the prosciutto on the pizzas. Garnish with basil.

PIZZA WITH TUNA & GINGER

This innovative pizza recipe comes from Japan, a country that has had an unparalleled love affair with pizza since the first Italian-American opened a pizzeria there in 1945.

MAKES TWO 10-INCH PIZZAS

½ cup julienned ginger

About ½ cup grenadine

6 ounces mozzarella, drained and sliced

2 crusts for 10-inch pizzas (page 231)

4 ounces fresh tuna, thinly sliced

Prepared wasabi to taste

Crushed red pepper to taste

2 cups baby arugula

Preheat the oven, with a baking stone in it if you have one, to 475°F for at least 30 minutes.

Place the ginger in a saucepan with ¼ cup water and the grenadine. The liquid should cover the ginger. If it does not, add grenadine until it does. Bring to a boil, then simmer until the ginger is soft and bright red.

Arrange the mozzarella on the two crusts, leaving the perimeters bare.

Place the pizzas in the preheated oven (or slide them onto the baking stone, if using) and bake until the crusts are golden, 10 to 15 minutes. Remove from the oven and arrange the tuna slices on the pizzas. Here the tuna has been coated with black pepper and seared (see page 47) but fresh tuna is also delicious. Place a dot of wasabi on each piece of tuna and top each portion of wasabi with a piece of ginger. Season with crushed red pepper, if desired, keeping in mind that the wasabi is hot. Mound half of the arugula in the center of each pizza.

FOCACCIA DI SOFIA

This type of cheese-stuffed focaccia hails from the Genoa area. It is a fun, rustic appetizer.
Serve it sliced into wedges on a wooden board with plenty of prosecco to wash it down.

MAKES TWO 10-INCH FOCACCIAS

4 cups 00 flour or unbleached
all-purpose flour

3 cups room temperature water

2 teaspoons active dry yeast

2 teaspoons salt

¼ cup plus 2 tablespoons extra-virgin
olive oil

7 ounces Robiola cheese

White truffle oil to taste

2 sprigs rosemary

Place the 4 cups flour in a large bowl. Measure the water into a measuring cup, then dissolve the yeast in the water and wait for it to foam.

Gradually pour the water with the yeast into the flour in a thin stream while mixing it with your other hand. When you have added about half of the water sprinkle in the salt and knead to combine. Gradually add the rest of the water in a thin stream and knead until you have a shaggy dough. Add the oil in a thin stream while kneading with your other hand. When the oil is combined, turn the dough out of the bowl onto a lightly floured work surface. Continue kneading with both hands until the dough is smooth, soft, and slightly tacky. If the dough is sticking to the surface or your hands, add flour in very small amounts. Shape the dough into a ball, return it to the bowl, and cover with plastic wrap or a dishtowel. Let the dough sit at room temperature until puffy and doubled in size, about 2 hours.

Preheat the oven, with a baking stone in it if you have one, to 475°F for at least 30 minutes.

Dust your hands with flour, remove the dough from the bowl, and divide it into two equal portions. Shape each portion into a ball, then use a rolling pin to flatten one ball into a 10-inch disk. Repeat with second ball of dough. Transfer the disks of dough to baking sheets (or a floured pizza peel if you plan to bake them directly on a baking stone). Use a fork or a skewer to poke holes all the way through the disks of dough.

Bake the focaccia until golden 10 to 15 minutes. Remove from the oven. With a serrated knife, slice each round of focaccia in half the long way. (Be careful as it is hot.) Use a spoon to remove some of the inner soft part of the two rounds to make room for the filling. Spread Robiola cheese on the bottom of each focaccia, then replace the tops and bake for an additional 5 minutes. Remove from the oven, drizzle with truffle oil, and garnish with rosemary.

CHOCOLATE SENSATION

Italy has had a long love affair with chocolate. In his 1778 book *La manovra della cioccolata e del caffè*, Vincenzo Corrado (Neapolitan author of the 1773 bestseller *Il cuoco galante*) covered these New World imports in great depth. Every restaurant needs one over-the-top chocolate dessert on its menu. At Serafina, this is a perennial favorite.

SERVES 4

1 cup cocoa powder

1 cup sugar

5 tablespoons unsalted butter

4 egg yolks

¾ cup unbleached all-purpose flour

3½ ounces white chocolate

5⅓ ounces dark chocolate

½ cup raspberries

Mint leaves for garnish

2 cups vanilla ice cream

Chocolate syrup for finishing

Preheat the oven to 400°F. Bring 1 inch of water to a simmer in a saucepan over medium heat. Place the cocoa powder, ½ cup sugar, and 2 tablespoons butter in a metal or heatproof bowl and place the bowl on the pot of simmering water to melt. Stir occasionally as it softens. Remove from the heat when only few bits are left, as they will melt from the residual heat. Remove from the heat and let the mixture cool for a couple of minutes. Whisk in 2 egg yolks and ¼ cup plus 2 tablespoons flour. Mix until well combined. Allow to cool 2 more minutes. Line an 8- or 9-inch tart pan with parchment paper and pour the chocolate mixture into the bottom. Bake in the preheated oven until soft but set, 25 to 30 minutes. Cool on a rack. Leave the oven on.

Bring 1 inch of water to a simmer in a saucepan over medium heat. Place the white chocolate, 2 tablespoons butter, and the remaining ½ cup sugar in a metal or heatproof bowl and place the bowl on the pot of simmering water to melt. Stir occasionally as it softens. Remove from the heat and let the mixture cool for a couple of minutes. Whisk in the remaining 2 egg yolks and the remaining ¼ cup plus 2 tablespoons flour. Mix until well combined. Allow to cool 2 more minutes. Line an 8- or 9-inch tart pan with parchment paper and pour the mixture into the bottom. Bake in the preheated oven until soft but set, 25 to 30 minutes. Cool on a rack.

When both disks are cooled, bring 1 inch of water to a simmer in a saucepan over medium heat. Place the dark chocolate and remaining 1 tablespoon butter in a metal or heatproof bowl and place the bowl on the pot of simmering water to melt. Stir occasionally as it softens. Remove from the heat.

Place the baked chocolate disk on a large flat plate. With an offset spatula, spread a thin layer of the melted dark chocolate on top. Place the white chocolate layer on top, then spread the remaining melted dark chocolate on the top and sides. To serve, cut into wedges and transfer to individual serving plates. Garnish with the raspberries and the mint leaves. Just before serving, add a spoon of vanilla ice cream on each plate and pour on the chocolate syrup.

TORTA DI MELE VERDI

Green Granny Smith apples are a natural hybrid of a wild apple and a cultivar invented in the nineteenth century in Australia by Maria Ann Ramsey Sherwood Smith. Granny Smith apples are wonderful in baked desserts, where their natural tartness mellows a little but still offsets the sweetness enough to achieve the perfect balance.

MAKES 5 INDIVIDUAL TARTS

CRUST

2 cups unbleached all-purpose flour

½ teaspoon salt

1 tablespoon sugar

1 stick plus 4 tablespoons unsalted butter

½ cup cold water

FILLING AND FINISHING

4 Granny Smith apples, peeled, cored, and sliced ¼ inch thick

4 tablespoons unsalted butter

½ cup sugar

5 scoops vanilla ice cream

5 strawberries, sliced

Mint leaves for garnish

LEMON ORANGE SAUCE

1 cup water

½ cup fresh squeezed orange juice

2 tablespoons fresh squeezed lemon juice

½ cup sugar

2 tablespoons unsalted butter

1½ tablespoons cornstarch

pinch of salt

For the crust, place the flour, salt, and sugar in a large bowl. Start kneading with your hands. When the ingredients are mixed, cut the butter into small pieces and add it to the bowl. Continue kneading for a couple of minutes, then add the cold water. Knead until the dough starts to come together, then move it onto a floured work surface, knead briefly, and shape into a ball. Wrap it in plastic and refrigerate for 1 hour.

Preheat the oven to 400°F and line a baking sheet with parchment paper. Remove the dough from the fridge and divide it into 5 equal pieces. Roll each piece into a 3½ -inch disk. Place the disks on a parchment-lined baking sheet and refrigerate for at least 15 minutes.

For the filling, arrange the apple slices on the disks, slightly overlapping in a fan shape. Cut the butter into pieces and dot the tarts with the butter. Sprinkle on the sugar.

Bake the tarts until the crusts and the edges of the apple slices are browned, 50 to 60 minutes. If the dough bubbles, poke the bubbles with the end of a chopstick to pop them.

Remove from the oven and allow to cool.

To make the lemon orange sauce, mix all the ingredients together. Cook, over low heat, stirring contantly until thick. Remove and cool before serving.

Just before serving, top each tart with a scoop of ice cream and garnish with strawberry slices and mint leaves. Drizzle on the lemon orange sauce.

INDEX

INDEX

ACKNOWLEDGMENTS

The making of this book was well and truly a celebration of the beauty of Italian cooking. The inspiration for this book came from Serafina's friends, family members, and patrons, who have been the very heart of Serafina's success over a quarter century of festive get-togethers, family reunions, and celebrations that underscore our global adventures.

Imagining a book to celebrate Serafina would have been impossible without Mark Roskams's beautiful, joyful photography. His images shine with the love and care put into every dish and transport the reader to the birthplace of each recipe, conveying the warmth of the afternoon sun shining on a corner of a dessert plate or the fragrant aroma of freshly baked pizza dough.

A very special thanks goes to Francisca Orihuela and Giulio Kleiner, who elaborated and transcribed the recipes for use in the home. We would also like to thank the many members of Serafina's restaurant teams who helped with the staging for this book. The same teams raise the bar at each Serafina location by preparing authentic dishes, serving specially sourced Italian ingredients with pride, and delivering homespun Italian recipes to Serafina's global and growing audience.

This book would not exist were it not for Serafina's food suppliers, whose products you will find in these pages. We want to acknowledge their dedication to quality, to preserving these national culinary treasures, and to perpetuating the principles of the Italian way of life. And, of course, we thank Jane Goldman, who believed in Serafina before anyone else did, and who embraced the dream.

Our deepest thanks go to Sabino di Biase and Luciano and Luca Ferrara, as well as Virginia and Alessandro Amati, for their hospitality at the wonderful Masseria Borgo San Marco in Puglia, and, of course, to Borgo San Marco's Rosellina Bonifacio for her creativity and generosity in showing us her skill in making fresh orecchiette pasta.

The book would not have been possible without the support of Antonia Jacchia in Milan and Silvia di Siena in Como; Elisabetta Papagni in Trani and Desideria Corsini in Porto Ercole. They opened their homes and their kitchens so that we could bring these dishes to life.

The team that put together this gorgeous project was led by Cristina Rizzo, whose palate and wit are the very center of this project, as well as by Rizzoli's Daniel Melamud, who guided the talented designer and editors at Rizzoli; without them this project would not be what it is today.

Thank you all for joining us in this celebration!